ALCHEMY

ALCHEMY

WRITTEN AND DRAWN BY

Oksanna Normandeau

Illustratrated by
Odara Rumbol

Alchemy copyright © 2022 by Oksanna Normandeau
All rights reserved.
No part of this book may be reproduced in any form
without written permission from the author.

Lyrics by The Beatles (*Eleanor Rigby*) - Pg. 2, *Routine*

Design & Layout by Rachel Clift.

ISBN: 978-0-578-36252-6 (Trade Paperback)
ISBN: 978-0-578-36253-3 (eBook)
ISBN: 978-0-578-38680-5 (Collector's Edition)

To my gorgeous Jacob
and sweet Cecilia,
none of this would have been possible
without you.

With all of my love,
endlessly.

ALCHEMY

al·che·my - /ˈalkəmē/

a seemingly magical process of transformation, creation, or combination.

ASLEEP IN THE MACHINE

i wake up

and put on my face

that is kept

in a jar by the door...

head out for my 9 to 5

complete mundane tasks to pass the time

drive home in rush hour traffic

eat dinner alone

rinse off the noise in the shower

fall asleep watching tv

repeat

day in and day out

where i am left wondering each night,

is there more to this life?

who is it for?

what i once thought i wanted

i now question

as to how it led me to such a place

overflowing with unfulfillment

am i just living

in my own disillusionment?

she caught my eye
in the midst of the chaos

stood out
like a green thumb

and i looked at her,
curious,
for the way she presented her scars

so daringly
while dressed in green and gold
fearless of her ability
to capture the eye of the beholder
and keep it

and sure enough
she looked back to me,
endearingly,
with a soft voice
vibrating through me

I am not here
to tell you
what your dreams are, my love

it is only my job
to help aid you in the process
of finding the true nature of your soul
so before I go
I must give you these

a gift
to you from me
in these dire times of need

I believe
you are distressed
by the destruction
down every path

but you are different from the rest
with answers hidden deep within
to lift the veil about why we are here together
sharing the same space

tree of life

unearthing new information
of old secrets

a wonderland of truth
just waiting to be seen

the thoughts
so profound
it causes the brightest of scholars
to crumble in the marvel
at the beauty
of the what if's it contains

but i must be still

for it takes time
to understand
the ineffability of the world
still remains

and it is
the unofficial way of life
to dance with the shadows

all these years

in an age of disinformation

to enter a time of over information

where i still do not know

left from right

or up from down

it turns out

i have been spoon-fed lies

from the day

i was born

the illusory

made to order existence

i grew up in

feeds on materialism

and capital gain

with weaponry

to dilute the most inner parts of ourselves

chemicals

social media

money

all moldings

to fit me into their box

normalcy

it is only now

as i escape the routine

of believing the world

was made to be convenient

that i see

what a matter of state

versus

what a state of mind

means

i mean,

how confusing to learn

the food i was taught provides nourishment

actually does more harm

than good

PESTICIDES
PROCESSED
FOOD
PRESERVATIVES

OHH MY

this idea has been
preciously placed in history

within each
lost and found civilization

but i have been refusing to acknowledge
what is in my mind's eye
for how to handle the problems

instead
i have found roundabout solutions
like powders and industry
to patch the wound
until it is no longer contained

a slow, painful
ending
like the plague

and my contribution
to the death of a society
whose physical scar on Mother Earth is so massive
it very well might be the last one to exist

(food for thought)

DARE

to use scare tactics

to frighten

an entire generation of beings

out of using natural substances

scientifically found

in our own bodies

(i contain controlled 1)

all of us

fools

to fall for their tricks
of the consensus
we are the dominant species
because we possess the ability to express emotions

look around

to those giant buildings
or the recently paved roads
impeding on the grounds below

we are living
in a constant hallucination
to think it is 'normal'
that when we look to the sky
we see no stars shining back at us

and it is imperative
we retreat to our roots
because we live in a plant's world
breathing life into existence
as they try to restore
what us humans
have wrecked with our ego
and when we go extinct
at the mercy of our own destruction
like our ancestors have shown before us

it will once again be
a plant's world

wonderland allows me to see

i am a wanderer

chasing the sunrises

and the sunsets

around and around

and around

trying to capture the essence

of why

i LOVE Mother Earth

so goddamn much

i can relay it to you

but at the end of the day

i am only left

with my memories

and these words

and i keep hoping

that it is enough for you to believe

in the universal magic of this existence

but i know in my heart

to fully understand

you must go around

chasing the sunrises

and the sunsets, too

sometimes

it feels impossible to express

the magic

when there is

imprisonment in language

censorship

and cancel culture

the masses are herded like sheep

while the truth is bent viciously

what once was free speech

is now a death sentence

comprised of hatred

and misconstrued interpretations

of what is

it really does make me question

if i should be putting myself out there

at all

(blind faith)

especially in places

where they teach you

how to act,

not how to think

for yourself

what has the world come to?
i ask the blue light

like i do not already know
as it plays
24 hours a day

i am sick
i yell

with disgust
with horror
with being a by-stander of hate

but

conflict fuels ratings
where fear feeds millions

and i continue coming back
every day.
waiting in the same line
for the same food
to fill my belly
and you would think
i would have learned by now
i will never be truly satisfied
from the over consumerism mentality
but here i am again

so whose fault is it really anyways?

(media)

little screen
little screen
what do you see?
is there another life for me?

inside that square box
of white sand beaches
filtered by
those pretty presets

little screen
little screen
what do you know?
does it truly show the glow?

in the physical life
does it actually matter
all the likes
and all the chatter

little screen
little screen
what do you think?
will there be a memory of me outside this rink?

or will this be my place
to take up space
for all of the things
i did achieve

(who knows)

what is natural

has been deemed taboo

what is cosmeticized

is now seen as the standard

for obvious reasons

greed to feed

the money machines

and now that i am aware

moving forward

all i want to figure out

is how much longer

am i going to keep allowing myself

to try and attain the unattainable

for their benefit

a hard change

when society's lesson on

how to be a woman

is telling me

stand up straight

no bodily functions

except tits out

and ass up

so i better watch my mouth

and my watch,

it better be the latest

that way i am not late

or too tall

or too blonde

or too flawed

but there is makeup

and creams

and lotions

and glittery things

to get me to feel confident enough

to wear those heels

and that dress

not too revealing

but just enough

though it is never enough

so i must go change

put on my smile

hide my hurt

push it deep down

without acting like it matters

and my act

well,

it better be convincing

it truly has caused me

to feel the need

to blame

to shame

to disrespect

the sacred flesh that carries me

in this physical journey

as i try to navigate my way

through the deception

and the pain

slowly losing connection

with each negative perspective

NOT GOOD ENOUGH
NAG
FAT
OVERTHINKER
BITCH
DEPRESSED
SHRILL
MOODY
DUMB
TEASE
WASTE OF SPACE
WEIRD
BOSSY
WITCH
STUPID
SILLY
TOO MUCH
LAZY
LOUD
UGLY
SHAMEFUL
WHORE

if you are constantly

emotionally surviving

you can never be truly

emotionally thriving

there is also

something to be said

about the pain

cutting so deep

i lose 10lbs

-i told them-

stop being

so dramatic

-they told me-

but i am hurting

-i said-

that feeling

of not being enough

strikes again

one problem fixed

another rearing its ugly head

around the corner

a creeping thought

the never-ending mediocrity

that

that is what

keeps me up at night

(sleepless in Seattle)

i just want them to see

all that i am

and all that i am not

and all that is

me

but all they want

is an act

put on for the public

with expectations about

who i am

what i am

how i am

while any deviation

from what is 'normal'

is unacceptable

crippling from a desperate need

to showcase my authenticism

but sold to the masses

stripped of my lifetime's hard work

dissected

used for parts

and then ridiculed

for every detail

which does not appease them

the allure of millions

of humans admiration

to feel loved

and accepted

at the sacrifice

of the parts

which make me, me

sad

how it has to be like that

(for fortune and fame)

who are they?

-to tell me how to live-

who am i?

-to decide anyone else's fate-

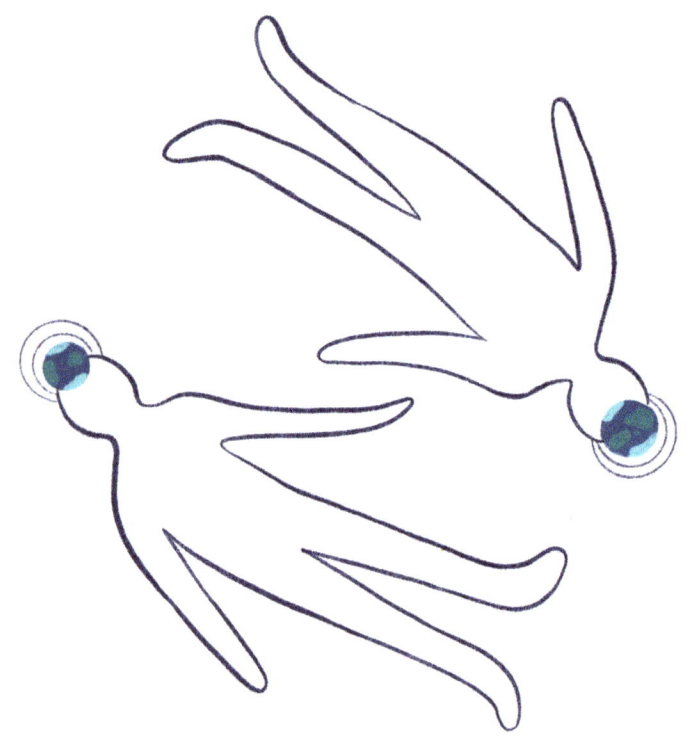

as they continue

to float through their existence

passing time with judgements

i understand

not everyone will agree

with my decisions

and i trust

they take any chance to

beat me into submission

with an iron fist

and a malevolent leader

laughing at my demise

(since they have already tried)

but i must continue

standing tall against

help me,

please

how do i learn to trust

when all i have witnessed

is the conspiracy against one another

forever left to decipher the truth

to fix a broken foundation

because today's confessions

do not change the years

of destructive forces

whose shots fired were so loud

it burst the eardrum

of those unfortunate enough

to be in range

help me,

please

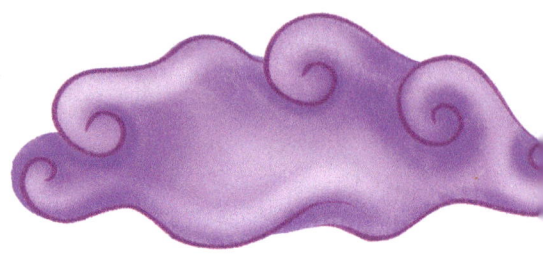

don't hold your breath . . .
don't hold your breath . . .

i know you want to
i know you want to believe
in a happy ending with humans
who have proved
they are capable of no such thing

you want to be the savior of sorts
to help them find their light
and let it shine
through the darkness they possess

but don't hold your breath . . .
no, don't hold your breath . . .

you cannot free the souls of those
whose shackles are still chained around their wrists
holding them hostage to the making of their own being

so don't hold your breath . . .
please, don't hold your breath . . .

the key they need to unlock themselves
from such imprisonment lies from within
as it does for you

*and maybe
you never see it*

*and maybe
it never happens*

*or maybe
it does*

*either way
you have the gift of choice
to act out of grace and compassion
towards their heart despite it all*

*so, breathe my love . . .
please, breathe my love . . .*

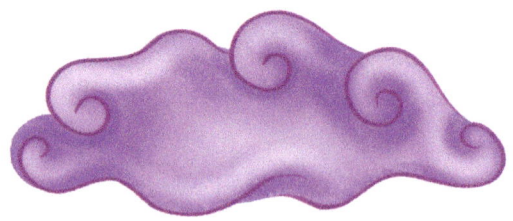

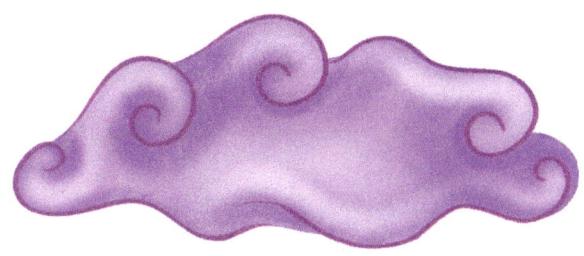

let the air flow through your veins

*let it take that fairytale notion
you can save all
and throw it out the door
so you can save yourself
before you get swept up in
someone else trying to*

just breathe . . .

*because it is so easy
to fall back into the temptations of the past*

*but if you keep repeating history
you are never going to last*

THE AWAKENING

the day
feels the same
as yesterday
yet different

the routine
has not altered

but somehow
the tea
is sweeter

the flowers
are more vibrant

the music beats
to the rhythm of life

and the love
oh, the love

it is all consuming

life must inherently be lived forward

for which i cannot see the outcome

yet can only be understood in steps backwards

for which i cannot relive

leaving my only option to be present in the now

for which is the only moment i can control

i feel slower

lighter

easygoing

not trying to rush the process

in a state of contentment knowing

i will get there

when i get there

where my only goal

is to be mindful of

each movement

every decision

all that life is

and is not

and finding my joy

in what it will be

i am searching to find

my peace

in love

in solitude

in being

or i might actually

lose control of my mind

so i will allow

my curiosity

to drive my intuition

as there is always

something, somewhere

waiting to be discovered

in wonder

to become wisdom

i turn inwardly

and dig deep

whilst asking myself,

WHAT IS

THE SILENCE

I KEEP?

there are

infinite perceptions

of me

millions

and millions

of versions

though

only i get to choose

which one

is projected outwardly

IN WITH THE GOOD SHIT

OUT WITH THE BULLSHIT

as simple

as it sounds

the most

powerful tool

i could teach myself

in this life

is how to

breathe deeply

i focus solely
on the breath
entering my belly

letting my chest rise
as i take in air
allowing it to circulate
throughout my entire body

i hold it at the top
without struggle

then exhale slowly
to release the internal noise
until there is a stillness
inside and out

peace and harmony
overtake my senses
and i use it
to prepare for my next cycle of breath
that takes me intrinsically deeper

(meditation)

just a little time

just a little space

just a little breathing

all for the sake

of a little bit of healing

it opened my eyes to see
my body has been speaking to me

it sends signals
like a cell phone
sends reminders

DRINK WATER

          EAT NATURAL

EXERCISE DAILY

          STRETCH ME

PLEASE

i was never taught
to listen intently to these
its call for help
for it has been diluted down
from the toxicity of the world

but now i know
with every choice to answer
brings me that much
closer to connection

(mind-body)

the body is the unconscious self

making the thoughts
in my head merely chatter

they are the automated response signals
from an overstimulating world

the power assigned to each one
will decide what has reigns over my conscious mind
ultimately constructing the presented self in reality

by acknowledging
and releasing them back
into the space outside the flesh

they eventually dissipate into the blackness
rendering them powerless

only then will there be
spaciousness from within

NOT GOOD ENOUGH
OVERTHINKER
TOO MUCH
WITCH
NAG
LAZY
SILLY
SHRILL
MOODY
BITCH
WASTE OF SPACE
STUPID
DEPRESSED
BOSSY
WHORE
SHAMEFUL
UGLY
TEASE

stillness —

it is here
and there
and everywhere

like the feeling
of the crisp air at 5am
when no one else is awake

or the chirping
of the birds
as the sun rises
through my window

in the way
i begin my day
with gentle yoga
instead of screen time

and the way
i end it
with a good book
instead of good booze

it is
the calm in the chaos
ready for me
wherever i am

(here, there, everywhere)

from morning to night

i continue my normal routine

but make my focus

the practice of letting go

everything that disturbs my peace

traffic

loud noises

spilled milk

any and all attempts

of bringing me out of the sereneness

is a chance to take a deep breath in

full of my emotions and exhale

to feel the calm course through me

and channel it into my reactions

then i will observe the way

the way the world changes around me

in a cosmeticized culture

it is easy to lose a sense of oneself

in all the material possessions

surrounding always

it provides a feeling

of false attractiveness

a deceptive little trick to the eyes

where if i add a little makeup here

and buy the latest tv for there

no one will know what hides behind

but what i have found is

the more things i have

the more things i have to worry about

and when i let down my guard

to the simple state of being

i was brought into this world with

a bare body

and a fire in my soul

there is not much more i need

(minimalism)

i will let go

i will let go

of my earthly desires

that only provide

tangible satisfaction

i will let go

of my wants

that deter me

from my needs

for the unique

individuation of the inner self

can only be achieved

by the breakdown

of the ego construct

i will let go

when i removed

apps

games

media

i gained

open eyes

presence

perspective

and it begs the question

for how much of this existence

i must have missed

because of a tiny dollhouse life

i carefully crafted

thinking it is real

instead of living in my reality

(technological thoughts)

300 chemicals

in my daily routine

between

hair

skin

makeup

and teeth

where never did i know

the damage below

until i set myself free

(no more products please)

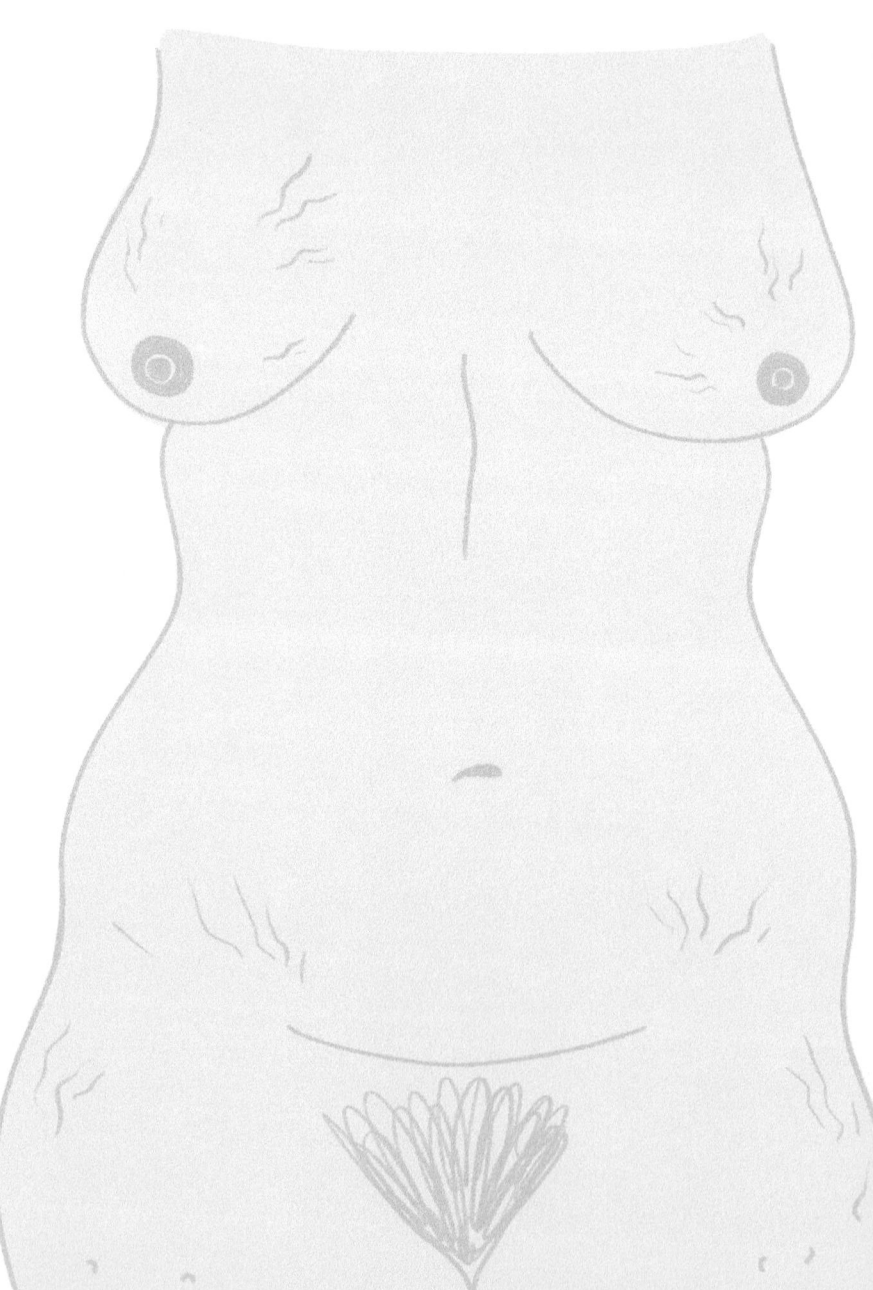

stretch marks

laugh lines

freckles

the flawless imperfections

of remembrance

of a life well-lived

it was when i got rid

of all the scent and flavor

that i let the natural taste

of honey drip from my lips

and it turns out,

it is so much sweeter

than sugar

(earthly)

the end is near

60 or so harvests left

i hear

until our food sources disappear

for then we will have nothing left to do

but fear

which is why

i want to live here

at the basis of it all

it is taking into consideration

the nourishment of my body

my food

my water

my warmth

and finding reliable sources

to create sustainable products

a symbiotic relationship

relishing the time

to experience

the seed of growth

and digging my toes

in the very dirt used

to sustain my existence

balance amongst species

creates

harmony throughout generations

believe me

i have been told
it is taboo to talk about
the naughty nipple
being brought up
in a society that thinks
the natural function of breasts
are only objects of pleasure
for the mouth of men
feeding on the nectar letdown

how disappointing
how we have become
shy to the reality
of their multifunctionality

where do you think
these men learned
to suckle each one
so tenderly at night

who kept their bellies full
and hearts warm
and souls comforted

where along the lines
did we lose respect
for the ones who

created us
carried us
cared for us

WOMEN
ARE GODDESSES

literal passages
for the spirit world
to come earthbound

a special kind of witchcraft
who can take one part of them
to create a whole tribe

without our due diligence
man would cease to exist
and this is my subtle reminder
to start acting like it

there are secrets of the universe

unveiling themselves

in these moments of sweet nothingness

and i continue

listening intently

as they open up to me

i have been given
the gift
of human connection

to embrace love
and the idea

we are one

with each interaction
is my choice

and i have decided
i am dreaming of life
in vibrant colors

where unconditional love
is the paintbrush of fruition

love needs no words

it knows

no boundaries
no race
no religion
no sexual orientation

it knows

no limits
no time of day
no location
no total amount

of ways one can express
how much the heart longs
for another

love needs no words

it is a feeling
easily reproducible
yet impossible to describe
unless allowed in
in its fullest capacity

like the feeling
of warmth
from the morning sun
kissing my skin

love needs no words

if love

is not the basis

to all my decision making

then how do I expect

to have a life

overflowing with it?

(what you give is what you get)

right now is the time

for self-reflection

taking a good look

and

asking the tough questions

magic mirror

before me

how can i

heal myself internally

for without deep deliberation

i walk through my life blindly

never giving myself

a chance to see the way self-love

was meant to be

at some point

during my philosophical rumination

i realized as much as i needed to let go

i also needed to let in

all of the lies

the deception

the misunderstandings

to feel them seep into my bones

and break under the pressure

drowning myself in the pain to understand

with each passing day comes healing

and only i can inspire my misery

i am the protector of my own peace

i am the protector of my own peace

i am the protector of my own peace

with my hands

over my heart

i whisper

i am

made of love

my heart

is overflowing

with love

i give love

freely

always

and then i

REPEAT

REPEAT

REPEAT

today

i choose
to walk away
from anything
that does not bring
joy into my life

i choose
to release myself
from the hurt
and the pain
and the coupled insecurities

i choose
to breathe slowly
from the place
of peace
from within me

i choose

to let in

the fruits of the spirit

to nourish

my aching flesh

i choose

to delve into

the natural healing processes

which comes

with an acceptance of self

i choose

to bring forth

the light i possess

to shine through the darkness

of that which surrounds

tonight

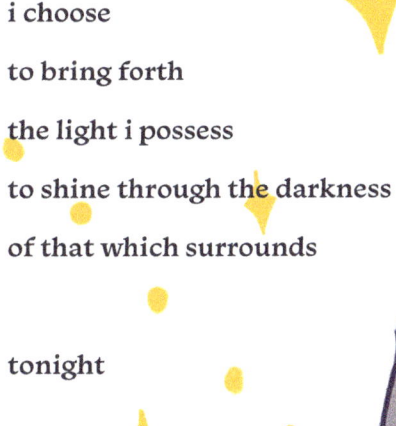

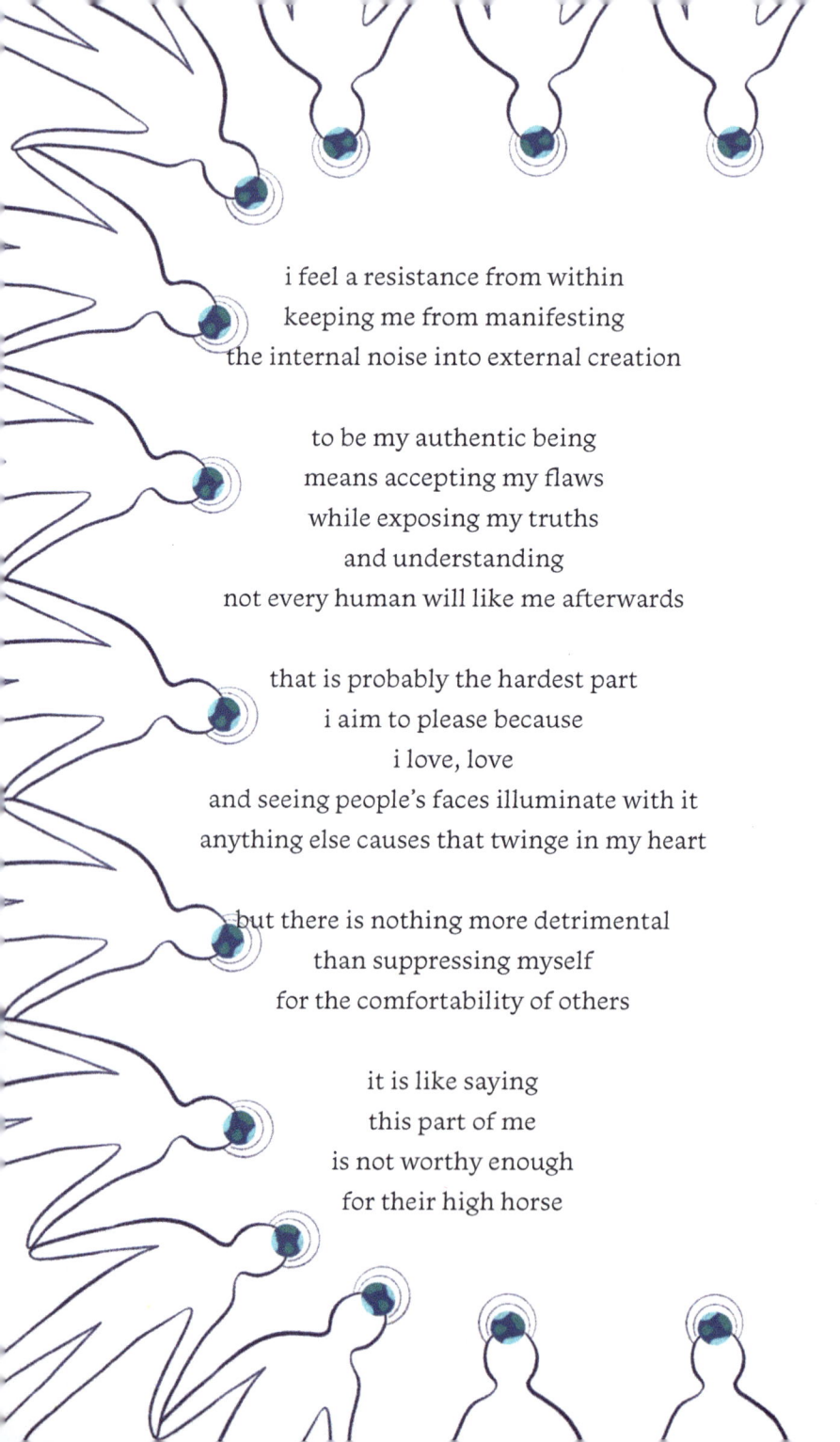

i feel a resistance from within
keeping me from manifesting
the internal noise into external creation

to be my authentic being
means accepting my flaws
while exposing my truths
and understanding
not every human will like me afterwards

that is probably the hardest part
i aim to please because
i love, love
and seeing people's faces illuminate with it
anything else causes that twinge in my heart

but there is nothing more detrimental
than suppressing myself
for the comfortability of others

it is like saying
this part of me
is not worthy enough
for their high horse

so let me treat me like a secret

    this quality
    or that trait
    or those characteristics

i will keep them hidden inside
    the darkest parts of me
      where it would be
the end of my world if they found out

    what a life
    to live out of fear
when there is no right way of being

so i say

i will move forward with what makes me happy
    and i hope you will do the same
      cheering each other on
        during the rise
    to our own versions of fame

(trepidation versus creation)

i have always believed
i am a girl
caught between the looking glass

on one side,
a sheep
trapped beneath
the weight
of the opinion
of others to keep up
an unrealistic image
of how i should be

designed for the system
molded to fit the bill
of an obedient soldier
willing to sacrifice self
for the comfortability of others

on the other side,
a goddess
wild and free
of incertitude
who runs with wolves
and speaks with conviction
unapologetic
about the truth
my heart yields

and the more i hear
the sweet sound of my inner voice
i am pulled deeper into my truth

the hardest part of the day

resides within the moment

of contemplation between

i should do this

and

i am going to do this

and i must remember,

i cannot become

if all i keep saying is

i should have done

express yourself

however you feel

makes you happiest

he told me

just promise

i will always have

a front row seat

(i promise)

writing is lovely

it waits like an old friend

i have been meaning to see

and when i do

it is like no time

has passed at all

always willing to pick up

right where i left off

to fill the empty spaces

where the silence is

i sat at the same
plastic covered window
with my pen and paper
day by day
staring at a simulated suburbia
with its freshly mowed lawns
and matching paint

i was waiting
for the words to come
to pour out of me
like a river in the spring

i sat and waited
for the inspiration
that takes the tongue
of writers who eloquently
display their souls
for good or bad

you know the ones
the isolationist types
who are married to their favorite spot in the house
with typewriters and a full pot of coffee
until the wee hours of the morning
making love to the pages beneath them

this is what i imagined i could be
what i would be

but the words never came

not even in the shred of hope
in the cherry blossom tree
solemnly waving to me in the wind
with her sweet pink
not even she
had something beautiful to say

and it was suddenly recognizable
the comfortable view from the movies
with everything i had ever known
picket fences, pensions, and social security
a life they tell you is worth living for

it would never hit the spot
like the way my lovers do
when they caress each crevice of my skin
and make it ache with pleasure

it would never provide
the same liberation that comes with
buying a flight with an hour notice
or skinny-dipping midafternoon in the blaring sun
or looking to the sky for stars
that are as far as the eye can see

the words would never come
if i continued
in the mundane elevator music of streets
who had never seen adventure
behind the red door of empty promises

my wild woman is powerful
i am the daughter of the moon
and a lover of the sun
day or night
light guides the path of my way
as i tune into my ajna
unveiling a different frequency of existence
to a higher consciousness
derived from the greater love above

my wild woman is liberated
i have the gift of tongues
and am warrior of the flesh
speaking my truth fiercely
to those in resonance with my energy
for within me lives
the spirit of the divine
the cosmic mother
of which all life sprouts
from the fertile soil of my womb

my wild woman is sacred
i transcend the human experience
and transform perceptions
for the awakening of the divine dimensions
in both the inner and outer realms
allowing the dualistic nature of the universe
to balance the flow of all primordial energies
around and through me
for the manifestation of oneness as a collective

over time

slowly

but surely

i have become

emotionally nude

and

i am loving

the view

for what felt

like an ending of self

was actually

the beginning of someone

i love even more

(my authentic being)

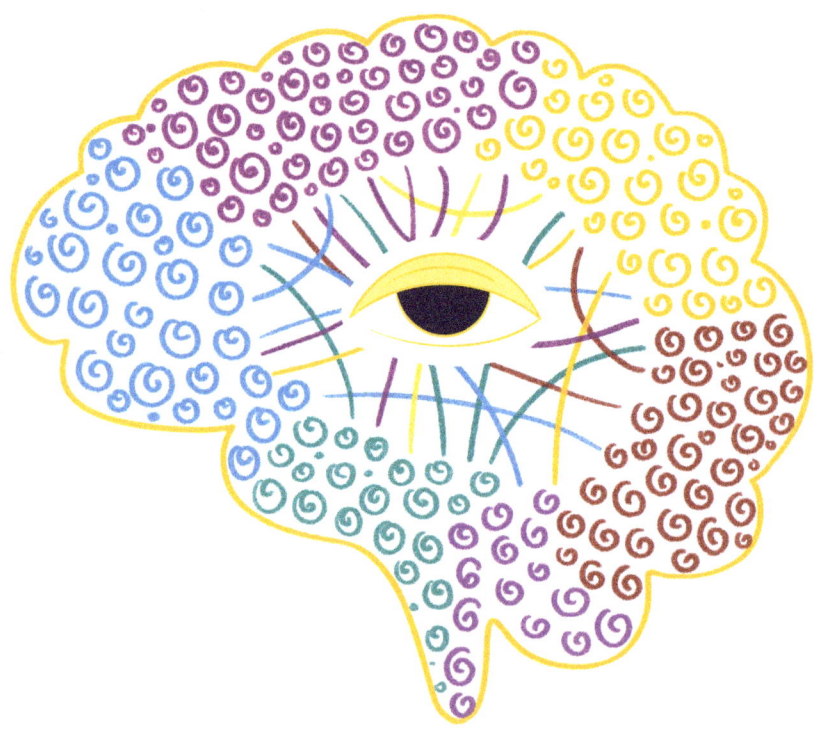

i had to rewire

my brain

to understand

the way others react

to me

is not a reflection

of me

(i am only in control of me)

the success of others

does not determine

the limit of my potential

just like their happiness

does not diminish

the light within me

and

vice versa

i will not be fooled

by the ways of the world

there is a chance

of facing adversity

in any task completed

so i plan to

run wild

talk freely

and ignite

the flame of my passion

wherever i decide

to invest my efforts

and each time

i fall off the wagon

once

twice

my 100th time

i will recover

i will not be afraid to start over

every. single. time.

for with

each loss

each hurt

each disappointment

i gain

more experience

more wisdom

more resilience

to succeed

and when i do

it will be

the most bittersweet taste in my mouth

knowing each time, i fell

i rose from my ashes

like the phoenix

i always knew i was

a wish

i wish

throughout my days

as i grow tall

amongst the wildflowers

is to stay curious

to rise with the sun

and howl at the moon

to explore the depths

and reach boldly for the stars

daring to believe

beyond what i can see

for the most beautiful thing

i can experience

in this life is the

mysteriously misunderstood

TRUST ME,

I THINK SO

INDEX

Asleep in the Machine

Routine

Disillusionment

Mother Earth

Open Eyes

Overthinker

Spoon-fed Lies

Pesticides, Processed Food, Preservatives, Oh My!

Food for Thought

DARE

Plant's World

Dreamer

Blind Faith

Modern Day Religion

Media

Little Screen

Cosmeticized

Society's Lesson on How to be a Woman

Blame Game

Surviving vs. Thriving

I Told Them

They Told Me

I Said

They Said

Sleepless in Seattle

Offerings

For Fortune and Fame

Who Are They?

Who Am I?

Everybody's in Their Own Worlds Anyways

Rebellion

Help Me, Please

Breath

The Awakening

Same Same but Different

Soren Kierkegaard Remastered

Contentment

Finding Myself

What is the Silence I Keep?

Perception

Breathe Deeply

Meditation

Just a Little

Mind--Body

Spaciousness

Stillness

Observation

Minimalism

I Will Let Go

Distractions

All-Natural

Flawless Imperfections

Honey

Self-Sustainable

Connection

Balance

The Naughty Nipple

Unveiling Secrets

The Biggest Secret of Them All

You

We Are One

Love Needs No Words

What You Give is What You Get

Winds of Change

Reflection

Realization

I am the Protector of my own Peace

Repeat

I Choose

Trepidation versus Creation

Looking Glass

Coulda, Shoulda, Woulda

Promises

Expression

Break-Through

Wild Woman

My Authentic Being

Rewired

Potential

Like a Phoenix

Find Adventure

Trust Me, I Think So

Seek Your Own Salvation

ABOUT THE AUTHOR

Photo by Brandi Greene @brandijeannephoto

Oksanna Normandeau was born in Lincoln, Nebraska but has lived in various places throughout the USA. One of the locations was Tempe, Arizona where she graduated from Arizona State University with a BA in Educational Studies. During that time, she met her (now) husband at a Taco Bell Cantina in Las Vegas. Their love was intense from the start and almost immediately fell pregnant with their first child, Cecilia. She is what brought Oksanna to the Pacific Northwest to be with Jacob where they currently reside together with new baby brother, Wayne.

Poetry was first introduced to Oksanna in childhood with Shel Silverstein's, 'Where the Sidewalk Ends'. It continued on into adulthood as she read through her semesters in college. It wasn't until her 20's that Oksanna went through one of my most influential transitions of her life where she turned to it for her own therapeutic means. She hasn't stopped writing since.

When Oksanna is not writing or drawing, you can find her hanging out with her family and friends. Her favorite pastime. She is also a professional, badass stay-at-home mom, wife, chef, maid, chauffeur, personal shopper, therapist, dry cleaner, etc. And when she has the time, she loves going on adventures like hiking, camping, and sitting amongst the wildflowers.

If you like what you experienced here, you can find more at -
  Instagram: @oncpoetry
  Tiktok: @oncpoetry
  Patreon: Oksanna Normandeau
  Etsy: ONormandeauCreations

ABOUT THE ILLUSTRATOR

Odara Rumbol was raised as a child in-between Sao Paulo, Brazil and London where she is now based. Free-spirited and creative Odara focused her energy on various artistic practices, which she developed at Ravensbourne university where she graduated in graphic design.

Influenced and inspired by such things as womanhood, feminism, nature, the unknown and magik. Her mediums of choice are illustration, painting, sewing and pottery.

You can find her eclectic body of work on Instagram @odararumbol

ACKNOWLEDGEMENTS

The people in my life are what I cherish most about this experience on Earth. Every moment spent together is never wasted time for me because I am my happiest when I am with all of them. Over the course of the past three years, the creation and birth of Alchemy took place. I was living and recording the pages you are reading right now. During that time there were individuals who entered my life and brought their energy and spirit to my work. They were the bursts of colors I saw while my face was pressed against the white paper. The meaning behind what I do and why.

If your name is here, know you had great impact on me and played a vital part in where I am today. I want to thank you from the bottom of my heart, and every other piece of it.

Thank you. Thank you for talking with me. Listening to me. Brainstorming. Laughing. Crying. Believing in me. Having faith in the journey and its destination.

Thank you for everything about you. For the time you gave me. The loved you shared. The deep conversations. The constructive criticism. The hard truths. Your smiles. Your thoughts and ideas. All of your joy and happiness and everything in between.

I am because of you.

Jacob	Kylie	Kailey	Grandpa Camp
Cecilia	Mikaela	Olivia	Uncle Bill&Deb
Wayne	Carly	Olyse	Brandi Bobby
Katrina	Ashley M	Mom	Preston
Ari	Ashley N	Dad	Susan
Devon	V&Z	Bob	Gabby
Britney	Jeannie	Meegan	Kaitlyn
Destinee	Odara	The Normandeau Family	Kenzie
Azure	Rachel	The Mulvahills	Elizabeth
Aussie Emily	Ariel	Uncle Josh	Loren

To my Insta fam –

The most badass writing community. We found each other in the darkness of the world and brought so much light into it together. Through collaborations, spoken word, poems, pictures, music, prompts, writing contests, giveaways, conversation, OUR ART. The most sacred manifestation of our beings and it was shared in love, respect, and enjoyment. You are a big reason why I have confidence and utter vulnerability with my work. I can't wait to meet you all in person someday.

To my Patreon fam –

The real OGs. Thank you for going the extra mile for me and believing in the dream from the beginning. Because of you I was able to fund this entire project and then some. I hope I made you proud.

To you, Dear Reader -

The journey was tough. With a lot of roadblocks and bumps, but we made it. Together. In love. In light. With a dash of magic. I hope you enjoy what you experienced and continue on future adventures by my side. Thank you for being here.

Last but certainly not least, an extra thank you to Odara and Rachel. For helping turn my paper thoughts and sketches into what you are holding in your hands. You made my dreams my reality.

www.ingramcontent.com/pod-product-compliance
Lightning Source LLC
Chambersburg PA
CBHW062049290426
44109CB00027B/2770